GOLD TO GOLD

BY THE SAME AUTHOR

Poetry
The Love Horse
A Partial Light
Our Ship
From the House Opposite
Feeding the Lake
In and Out of the Apple
Homing
Depending on the Light
Selected Poems
For the Moment
Counting the Chimes: New and Selected Poems 1978-2003
The Other Day
The Point of Loss
Treatment
Gestures and Counterpoints

For children
Once there were Dragons
Boo to a Goose
The Mad Parrot's Countdown
Catching the Spider
The Conjuror's Rabbit
Back by Midnight
Hot Air
The Dummy's Dilemma
Copy Cat
The Wonder Dish
This is the Blackbird
All the Frogs

Libretto
Alban; a community opera

Criticisn
Passing Judgements

GOLD TO GOLD

JOHN MOLE

Shoestring Press

Printed by imprintdigital
Upton Pyne, Exeter
www.digital.imprint.co.uk

Typesetting by narrator
www.narrator.me.uk
info@narrator.me.uk
033 022 300 39

Cover design by Ellen Kydd
EllenKydd.com

Published by Shoestring Press
19 Devonshire Avenue, Beeston, Nottingham, NG9 1BS
(0115) 925 1827
www.shoestringpress.co.uk

First published 2020
© Copyright: John Mole
© Cover image: John Mole

The moral right of the author has been asserted.

ISBN 978-1-912524-53-2

ACKNOWLEDGEMENTS

Some of the poems in this collection first appeared in the following publications: *Allegro, PN Review, The High Window, The Rialto, The Spectator, Stand*, and in the pamphlet *A Different Key* (New Walk Editions).

For
Simon and Ben

CONTENTS

THE COUNTER-DRIFT

Drifting downstream against the current
you wonder at first how this can be
unless some instance of magical thinking
has for the moment set you free
from every quotidian constraint
and the drag of familiarity.

Then as your journey gathers pace
you take for granted this counter-drift
and follow its liberating course
wherever it leads, as your spirits lift
with the buoyancy of sheer surprise,
and never a thought of sinking.

THE REBUKE

Driven by language, as a pianist
by the sight of ivories, and restless
when not at the keyboard
improvising word after word
to discover myself, I seldom
held back. Poetry was the momentum
and melody of my being,
always either on song or clearing
my throat for it. Arpeggios
in search of resolution, one phrase
chasing another, the delight
of never having to wait
for voice or accompaniment
to find its match in the imminent
and likely poem
      Which is why now
in bereavement's wake, the undertow
of loss, I fear the doldrum drift
from one false start to another, to be left
behind by what was once
the creative certainty of chance
that drove me. When I look
at what I have written, its rebuke
is that such conscious effort
should seem so lifelessly apart
from impulse, that such wordiness
should seek for reassurance, and that loss
has yet to lighten, finding the way
to make fresh music in a different key.

MEMO: AT THE WORKDESK

The welcome irritant
of a word cluster
easing itself
into clarity, becoming
what it had intended
before arrival
and so by expansion
setting out.

*

Where you go
had better not be
where you went
last time
but where discovery
now leads you
with the momentum
of surprise.

*

Relish amazement
for its sudden
brief duration,
for the miracle
of getting something
so exactly right
that celebration
must be to start afresh.

TO THE READER OVER MY SHOULDER

Let there be approval
in the weight of your chin
as it rests so close to my ear
that each breath you take
is held for longer
than I dared expect.

May what I have written
be the best I can manage
to surprise us both
with the truth of it all
as you press down hard
and whisper *Yes.*

THE BIRTH OF A POET

At his grandparents' house in Rochester, John Ashbery had his
first 'unexpected encounter with a word' (sitting on the landing
one day, he suddenly thought: *I regret the stairs*).
– Karn Roffman, *The Songs We Know Best*

Caught between meaning and sound
and ambushed by both
as he sat between them,
those stairs were his first poem,
complete, far from regrettable
in the sudden surprise
at discovering a world of words
to be unexpected. All else
would come later, the syntax,
the craft, the body of work,
the playful enlargement
of ambiguities, the published
reputation. For now
one syllable was enough
to be carried in secret
like an unbroken promise,
back down into the hall.

1944

Staplegrove, Somerset

A haystack's gold block
was the currency
of wartime innocence.

In an open field
where I walked with my mother
its thatched bulk comforted.

At the end of our road
we watched the Yankee soldiers
as they marched to camp.

They too were company.
The way they whistled
and the songs they sang.

*

Run, rabbit, run
across the keyboard
of Charlie Kunz,

our family favourite
always on the wireless
chasing Hitler.

And sometimes as a treat
it was rabbit
for dinner on Sunday

full of the shot
that could break a tooth
but not your spirit.

*

On Mr. Nash's farm
it was always Winston
I asked to see.

Gloss-flanked, snorting
barrel of a boar,
he lifted his wet snout,

poked through the wire,
nuzzled for acorns
from my overcoat pocket.

It's a cigar he's after
my father would say
and Mr. Nash would laugh.

*

What we needed was
a needle in that haystack
for sewing nametapes,

save and mend,
with a wooden mushroom,
darning socks,

and there were names like
Chilprufe and Viyella
to keep me warm,

but the Ration Book
wasn't for reading
at least not by me.

*

Tripe was what the papers
wrote a load of
roared my father

at the breakfast table,
bringing his fist down
on our chequered cloth,

then, as a mild reply,
my mother served it up
at suppertime

when nothing much else
was in the larder
so it had to do.

*

Surely you can't remember
any of this, they insist,
you were far too young.

But invention is the child's
gift for vividly recalling
what he has been told

and who is to say
it wasn't exactly so
before I found the words?

Four years old is already
a storehouse of impressions.
Believe me, I should know.

PIT STOP

1945

My tin-can pedal car
clanks across the gravel

towards Dad's shed
for his attention.

Among the rags and shavings
stands our family mechanic.

It needs oil, he says,
reaching for the 3-in-One.

            *

Driving away, thumbs up,
a neophyte competitor

in Startrite shoes
and pulled-up socks,

I leave the pit stop
for a world elsewhere,

my mother waving
from our kitchen window.

THE SOCKS

To pull his socks up
was what he was told

as he lived each day
without due care,

grazing his knees
on a common playground

and laughing aloud
at the straight and narrow.

                 *

Then there came a day
when it wasn't enough

for the socks to remain
around his ankles

so he pulled them up
and there they stayed

whether or not
of their own accord.

STARTING OUT

Walking back home
at a child's pace

with his mother, hand in hand,
as if starting out

all over again, forgetful
and eager, forgiveness

like the ring she wears
felt for and held tight.

                     *

Call it, if you will,
a return journey,

the route prepared
by guilt and love,

each precious resolution
marked along the way

until they reach
the instant of his birth.

SMALL MERCIES

She lived at Wit's End
in a house called Small Mercies.

On a quiet night
it let her sleep.

Sometimes she dreamt
that life was for living

and when she woke
she just had to believe it.

                        *

Either that
or a stony silence

weighed her down
where she lay her head.

Pillow talk
was a long conversation

she took no part in
for good or ill.

THE MISTLETOE SHOW

Always hung up last thing
as if to kiss were the most daring,
the most not quite
proper behaviour on that sacred night.

It had to be full on the lips,
not just family fellowship's
chaste peck but a passionate
reminder which had been worth the wait.

She would watch him shyly
while he tied the knot, occasionally
glancing at their children then away
as if such love-play

needed innocent witnesses
to what was hardly less
than all that either could do
to hide it, a hullabaloo

of eagerness, restraint
and expectation, both of them intent
on what must follow, the tense
theatrical balance

of his stepping down, how he'd stand
beside the chair, one hand
to steady him, the other
reaching out to her

until with a sudden
rush of seasonal abandon
so exactly matching his
she would seal their Christmas kiss.

AUGUST FOR THE BOYS

A hard time we had of it
in those glory days of summer.
Cricket, we were bad at it
and tennis was a bummer.

Swimming was too strenuous,
Golf was too expensive,
Sex might have made men of us
but the course was too intensive.

Guides were not our cup of tea,
au pairs unobtainable,
and holidays beside the sea
were frankly unsustainable.

The English Riviera snored,
Blackpool was overrated.
The truth is we were mega-bored,
scruffy and acne-plated.

A hard time we had of it,
no highlights to remember.
Autumn, we'd be glad of it.
Roll on September.

ADMISSION

Cambridge 1960

Summoned by the Tutor for Admissions
to be inspected at this
as yet unfamiliar College
where a brace of pheasants
hung from a courtyard window
and an avuncular air of deference
hung in the Porter's Lodge,
I stood there admitted,
just inside his door
waiting for him to speak.

                At first,
theatrically framed
between imitation porticos,
in tweed plus-fours,
preoccupied, absorbed
by important business,
he went on picking
at a fly, attaching it
to a line from the long rod
angled across his knee,
until, as if distracted
by collegiate procedure
and by what I must be there for,
Do you fish? he asked,
almost too casually
for the question to be a trick
or snare. *No, but my uncle does*
I replied, as if the truth
were failure at one remove.

               Which is all
I can now remember
of what must have been

an interview of sorts,
and myself a catch neither
destined for High Table
nor small enough
to be thrown back in the river.

ON A PAINTING BY GRANT WOOD

For Susan Friesner

We, the daughters of the revolution,
invite you to join us for tea
and an opportunity to put this world
to rights according to the next
on which we have firm opinions,
praise the Lord. There will be no judgement
to which we shall not rush, no cushions
on our high-backed chairs, since virtue
sits upright and comfort confuses
the mind and spirit. We shall offer you cake
but expect you not to eat it, acknowledging
the domestic formalities even as we deplore
the sweetening of sugar. We stare at this
uninvited artist, this interloper
who returns our reflections, reassembling
the shards of a broken mirror
according to his ways and means
which are certainly not those of the Lord.
God bless America. We hold it in trust
like the finest bone china between
fastidious fingers, our gaze
remorseless, our determination
the set of a collective jaw
against all who would question
our values. There is so much we need
to put you straight about before
the men return as it seems they always do
in the end. So the time must be now
or never. Let us begin…

A BRIEF ENCOUNTER IN THE BROCKET ARMS

Our local Ladyship with an entourage
of two young men, both gloriously effete,
(and she in furs, unwithered by old age)
has made her entry. Ready to greet
the marvel of this rare event as theatre
mine host acknowledges their approach,
placing three glasses on the bar
in readiness, but upstaged by his pooch,
a playful jet black Labrador, he watches
while she sniffs the trio, making her choice,
(It is, of course, My Ladyship she chooses)
then stands on hind legs, covering a face
from which with thespian relish comes the cry
Is this bitch on heat, sir, or am I?

THE VICOBOLD

For Peter Scupham

The slap and clank
of start-up, ink

applied, not slab
but thick enough, a dab

of oil from your old tin
long-beaked can

on the big wheel's
axle. What else?

Tighten the chase,
hammer and press

one last time, bed
loose slugs, unsettled

or uneven lines,
check all four quoins

then pass the poem
over to the hum

of readiness, insert,
adjust, make straight

and line by line
admire the good work done,

stand back, lean in
for the wheel's lugubrious spin

19

to gather speed
as each laid sheet

is printed, stet,
unchangeably displayed.

GRINDSTONE

Accelerate the pedal
to a roaring spin

then place each
blunted blade exactly,

press it down
and watch the sparks fly

upward, outward
as the dull edge sharpens.

        *

Let what is ineffectual
find its point,

the fire, the flint,
the grip, the flight,

my father's shed become
creation's galaxy,

a darkness filled
with glittering rust.

POTTERING

Moving at random round the house
was what my elderly father did
as I do now. He called it
pottering, not going anywhere
with a purpose other than
to be occupied, to take, as he said,
his mind off things. I'd hear him
open a door then close it without
entering the room, or watch him
try a switch just to make sure
the light was working. 'What
are you up to, Dad?' 'Oh nothing much
that couldn't have waited, but now
is as good a time as any.' It was
and is, as I reach out to put an arm
around his shoulder only to find
that it's my son's affectionately
laid on mine. 'What are you up to, Dad?',
announcing his arrival as, with matters
to attend to, my father wanders off.

DROUGHT

The cracked face of exhaustion
is not that of an old friend
gone finally to earth. It stares up

from the bed it lies on,
a familiar stranger
thirsty for water and love

BECALMED

You hold a finger up
to where the wind should be
then raise both hands
for nothing. All at sea,
alone, directionless
in a wide silence
beneath the rigging,
you remember how once
you journeyed with ease
across brisk waters,
following a course
that always answered
to the wind in your sails,
outward bound then
safely home again,
but now no sight of land,
no guiding star,
not even a whisper
of who on earth you are.

ON EARTH

Where on earth
are you? Your mother's
playful childhood cry
when you were wanted
back in from the garden,
or your late wife's call
less playful, too much
work to be done
about the house,
but now as you sit alone
and hear their voices
reaching across
the gulf of absence
in a counterpoint
of love and recollection
you reply to both
with *Here I am*
on earth, and still
with work to do,
my daily keeping
of the promise made
and held in trust for you.

HIS FAMILY HAS BEEN INFORMED

Summer's here at last. The guttering
has been repaired, so all we need
is a storm to test it. Not long now
if the year so far is anything to go by.
The garden's started to look good.
I've kept up with the cutting back
and the kids both do their best to help.
Mum and Dad came over yesterday.
We watched the lunchtime news together.
Mum said too much politics
and Dad went on about how you can't believe
a word they say, but neither of them
lets me turn it off. Sometimes
it's on all day. I'm anxious if there's no report
and frightened if there is, but at least
the sun came out. We'd arranged a barbecue
but couldn't get the coals to light
so I had to use the oven. Done like that
it never tastes the same. We needed you,
your outdoor touch. *A man about the house*,
said Mum, which didn't please my father
but at least he laughed. What else?
Remember we put our names down
on the allotment waiting list?
Last week a plot came up and I've taken it.
You should see me marching off
with all the gear. Just like that Land Girl
on those old posters, digging for victory,
keeping calm and carrying on.
I like the company up there.
Everyone seems friendly, asking about you
and the children, and giving me advice
on what to plant and when. There's even a committee
but not too formal, nothing to make you feel
you're back on parade, I promise you,
although our chairman, as he calls himself,

rather reminds me of the sergeant-major
in that silly film we used to watch.
Anyway, by the time you're home
a few green shoots at least should have appeared,
and they'll all be mine to greet you!
I count the days to go before your leave
and cross them off, each mark on the calendar
a kiss of course. So nothing more to tell
except I love you which is hardly news
though it makes *my* headlines. Must go.
Supper to get, then the kids' homework.
They send their special hugs.
We probably ought to water the garden
but I think tomorrow it may rain.

DREAMING OF THE THIRD MAN

Harry Lime approaches me in longshot
across the Prater, at first a dot
as if seen from above, then clearly defined
by his coming closer. I know this will end
with our meeting face to face. It must be the same
projected trick of memory, a shared dream
scripted by love, and by the film you and I
watched so many times together before we
visited Vienna. Smiling, Harry has news
that makes me weep with happiness
and expectation; *Old man, your wife*
is waiting there at the foot of the wheel, alive
as she was that time you looked down
at her, seated and patient, while the huge frame
carried you up without her. She had been too nervous
to come too, remember? Yes, Harry, of course,
as if I could ever forget. How at such a height
so suddenly without her I could hardly wait
for touchdown when, embracing each other
as if for the first time, we almost ran together
back to the hotel and nakedness, made love
then lay there as I do now but alone. Harry, save
this memory for me. Though I have to wake
return to me soon in sleep, a precious outtake
from the film that haunts my dreams again and again,
each time differently, each time the same.

DIAGONAL

This is the way I must lie now
as I enter your space at an angle
in the double bed we shared.
Move over you would have said
but come to me later
as, look, I have done already,
embracing absence
like the lost half of a kiss
gone missing somewhere
across a deep divide.

I sleep in this vacancy
for both of us, so hold me
until I wake, and then until
I come back after another day
to how it always has to be
when loss and desire
lie down together.

GOLD TO GOLD

I wear your ring now
on my left hand's little finger,
the two of us together
side by side who never made it
to our fiftieth anniversary
but celebrate each day
by touching gold to gold.

Cold weather is the fear
of losing you a second time.
my ring embedded,
yours less so, reminding me
how beautiful your hands were,
slim and reassuring
as they lay on mine.

THE VALLEY

All's now temperate in this
familiar valley of loss.
At home here, as day
dissolves into day, I balance
memory and hope to measure out
not grief or expectation
but companionable pain.

If the mind has mountains
mine are scaleable
and intimate, their shadows
patching the landscape they
glow with patience. So this
is world enough and time
or must be while it lasts.

A PREMONITION

i.m. Edward Thomas

Who was it that cleared his throat
to what end? With something to say
before he thought the better of it
and settled back in the only way

of being a ghost? Let birdsong,
risen above all incidental sounds,
leave its crescendo with the living
as music is a wordlessness which mends.

Besides, what would be broken
other than his heart by hearing said
all that he could utter of those men,
his travelling companions, the dead

he now belonged with? Life
best left for those with time to dream
their onward journey, and grief
a bare platform, a hiss of steam.

FOLK FESTIVAL IN A CHURCHYARD

For Kenneth Padley

Shadows there on the flint wall,
ink-black silhouettes much
larger than in life, reach
out to each other. Who can tell

that light is not playing tricks
or that a well-aimed beam
has not now usurped the moon
and the hands of the church clock

gone into reverse? These
could all be ghosts relieved
of their whiteness, the loved,
the lost, returned to praise

this annual gathering -
stranger, neighbour, friend
who wander on sacred ground
to drink and dance and sing.

GOING HOME

Folk Festival

Closing her last set
she sings of going home
while couples rise up
from the bales they share
to fold into each other's arms
already spirited
across love's threshold,

then later as I step
alone into our house
I think of us as the song
must have me do
on this dusky, scented
summer night
that still belongs to you.

IN THE BUTTERFLY HOUSE

As I pass through, flutterings brush
against me, settle a moment on my shoulder
before I leave. *A word in your ear*
they seem to whisper, *then make a wish*
that our beauty and weightlessness
might be sufficient, that wings may unfold
and close in safety far across the world
before it becomes too late. On leaves
and bark and exotic bloom
the iridescent miracles alight
then, seeming to think twice, take flight
as if this crowded, temperate room
were not the sanctuary it appears
but a honey trap. Frail specks,
they cluster against the glass and perspex
carrying with them all our fears
on their behalf. Amazed, informed,
I read and then forget the Latin names
but what they come to signify remains
in stark translation: *You have been warned.*

THERMOSTAT

He really has no thermostat
you said of our friend
whose take on life
was the heat turned up
and his boiler roaring.

Such lavish gifts,
such boundless generosity,
such exhaustive wit.
A gradual radiation
overwhelming the room.

Then after each visit
for a while we'd leave
a window open,
letting his disappearance
cool us down.

THE HUMPTY DUMPTY STAMP-LICKER

Yellow legs akimbo, slapping fat thighs,
perched on a water-drum with two pop eyes,
when you twist the cap on its porcelain crown
this ridiculous egg won't tumble down
but sticks out its tongue from a mouth so wide
that it almost splits the shell from side to side,
then you twist again, the tongue goes in
and leaves you with the open wound of a grin.
It sat on my grandfather's writing desk,
no less functional than grotesque,
but now it's on mine by inheritance,
watching me write. Throw it out? Not a chance.
I know its dried-up uselessness
is a bond between us that we daren't express.
There's a look of horror on its painted face,
its parched tongue gags and stays in one place,
its water drum is empty, its bulbous head
twists to no purpose, becoming instead
a sort of eccentric memento mori
as we gaze at each other, eye to eye,
waiting for an envelope that will not stick
with nothing inside and no stamp to lick.

THE PUNCH AND JUDY PUPPETS

For Simon

Mr. and Mrs. Punch
are selling up, so it's farewell
to the narrative's menage
as one by one the puppets
desert an empty booth,
their occupation gone.

The last of them to leave
is the lonely policeman
after his farewell beat
where everyone behaves
because all trouble
has moved on out of town.

Mayhem is now elsewhere
under new management
so good dog Toby
sniffs at a lamp-post
then trots accommodatingly
out of the picture.

Where there was once
a string of sausages
dragged from the butcher
there is now only
a patient, orderly queue
at the meat counter.

The baby has ridden off
on the crocodile's back
en route for
the Peaceable Kingdom
where all must be disrupted
by their arrival.

As for the hangman
with his knotted rope
not to speak of the devil
we're better off without them
though in our wildest dreams
that's still the way to do it!

BLY

The Turn of the Screw

Where are they now, the governess
you dreamed you were before you fell asleep,
the perfect gentleman, the little miss,
the snuffed-out candle, passionate kiss,
and all the locked-in secrets that you keep?

Never believe that they will not be there
still waiting when you wake, the echo of your needs
in two enduring images, fierce with desire:
Quint on the tall tower's topmost stair
and gaunt Miss Jessell watching from the reeds.

LIKE CASABLANCA

This is where beautiful friendships always begin
and the usual suspects are rounded up,
where the private getaway plane is waiting
for the two of us, just a kiss and a small step
across the tarmac. But hurry, that jeep
will arrive on cue, and the mist we were lost in
thicken to night and fog. And then what hope
for the last-minute take-off, for anything.

How exquisite the nostalgic ache, the promise
that suddenly our song will be remembered
in a bar in Berlin or London or Paris
where we'd met by chance, where we first heard
the news of what would become of us
and you smiled, telling me not to believe a word.

AT A LITERARY PARTY

When the exquisite corpse was offered wine
he was happy enough to make do with water,
nor did he go for the vol-au-vents
or the cheese and olives on little sticks.

He moved with gusto among the guests
who raised full glasses to his bones
but when he challenged their opinions
they saw right through him and told him so.

Since yesterday's man had been invited
the two of them sought each other out,
comparing notes on the afterlife
and the column inches of reputation.

Then they left together in a taxi -
Where to, gents? the driver enquired
but when he turned round both seats were empty
and the ticking meter was all he heard.

HACKED

Find the body where it fell.
All is very far from well.
This is a story that will sell.

No time to take a second look.
Fresh bait dangles from the hook.
Someone must be brought to book.

Messages remain unread.
Listen in on them instead.
Postscript echoes of the dead.

Search the neighbourhood for a clue.
Fact or fiction? It's down to you.
Any subterfuge will do.

Gather reports and hold the page.
Release them slowly stage by stage.
Suspects, friends, their sex, their age.

This is a story that has sold.
Now for the next plot to unfold.
Grief is worth its weight in gold.

ON THE TRAIN

En Avant

Doors open for debouchment
and admittance, close, then

open again experimentally
to prove their closure

fit for purpose while the tannoy's
litany of stations and the hiss

of brakes releasing
are a complementary prelude

to the main event, libretto
and orchestration, *en avant.*

Verbal

Sounds as if he got away with it
whoever it was came up

in this angry jiggering exchange
between two whippet-thin

St. Vitus dancers with their beer cans
at the carriage door too long in opening.

One to the other. *It was like
who are you looking at, you fucker?*

*I didn't give him what I should've done.
I only give him verbal.*

After Work

I wasn't having any of it.
I told him where to go.

Their hostess suits identical,
their smartphones too.

What an arsehole!
Will he be in tomorrow?

One sends a text.
The other enquires who.

Believe me. Really
you don't want to know.

Loner

Calling up a spreadsheet
on his tablet, studying

the graphics of anxiety
or triumph, *Right,*

he mutters to himself,
this time it has to be

then hums a few bars
of 'Story of my Life'

by New Direction
as he switches off.

Between Stations

Stopped here for half-an-hour
and no one has said a thing.

Several times the carriage
has groaned and juddered

and people have looked up at each other
then returned to their screens

or removed their earphones,
shrugged and put them back.

One girl takes a selfie, and *woosh*
she texts it to a friend.

An Elderly Couple

Side by side, in the after-glow
of a special occasion,

he has an opera programme
in his lap, and she

her shining handbag.
Sleepy? We'll soon be home.

She yawns demurely
into the back of her hand.

The discretion of his fart
is a joy to behold.

Feet up

A copy of *Metro* folded
on a vacant seat, *Excuse me*

is that your paper?
Have you finished with it?

Affirmative. He reaches over,
spreads out a double page,

lies back, and like a dreamer
shooting his cuffs

extends immaculate shoes.
His socks are purple.

Only the Best

Both of them it turns out always
shop at Waitrose. Comparing lists,

how easy it is to find the best
at reasonable prices,

their gossip is a shrill exchange
of quality and praise.

One: *They're all so friendly*
at the checkout. The other: *Yes,*

 and where else could you hear a mother say
'Just put that kumquat down, Orlando!'?

47

Wired

The nodding head,
the tintinnabulation

of plugged-in earphones,
yeah yeah yeah

and wired
to the pocket

where one free hand
delves and fumbles

while the other
gropes his girl.

Short Distance

School tie loosely noosed,
the uniform of not being

one of you or bothered,
she makes a call

to her friend only half-way
down the compartment:

Come here a minute.
Gary doesn't believe me.

A bundled commotion
barging up the aisle.

End of the Line

Life gathers its belongings
and prepares to move on.

This train terminates here.
Briefly the platform is crowded

then a few are left
staring at timetables.

Where now? Where next?
Or is the return journey

already paid for
to start all over again?

REMEMBERING CLEO

Snug in the crook of my arm
you'd shift as we lay together,
one paw languorously extended,
hypnotised by your purring
into absolute content.

I'd watch those beautiful owl eyes
narrow then shut then again
open less wide until a last yawn
closed on silence, yours, mine,
and we went our separate ways.

OPEN GROUND

The one who sings is not always happy
– Pierre Bonnard

To sing nevertheless
whether under your breath

or buoyantly aloud
full-throated

is a choice not given
to silence

in the shadows
cast by fear of loss.

               *

So let where you sing
be open ground

as all must await
the song's arrival.

Melodious sunlight
spreads from leaf to leaf

and note by note
recovery begins.

FULL MEASURE

She takes his empty glass
and holds a finger to her lips

as if to silence him
or keep a secret.

He remembers how she did this
in another life

before it suddenly became
the one they shared.

*

And how the glass
between them on the table

filled with love-light
as her moistened finger

circled its rim
to make such music

rising to a pitch
that measured his desire.

PASSING

Adrift in the element
of pure thought

between recognition
and memory,

she reaches out
to all that will pass

already fading
as it disappears.

*

Stopped for a moment
by the light of her eyes,

an outstretched arm,
that buoyant hair,

time insists on beauty
still floating there

in the afterglow
of her sudden passing.

COMMA

Not a boomerang or a frisbee thrown
in the expectation of return
but a careless comma loosed mid-air
on a breezy page, insouciant,
experimental, to see how it flies
and where it lands, the fresh ground
chanced upon, choosing not to settle
any place it has before. Or otherwise
the deliberate one that made his day
for Oscar Wilde when he removed it
from a sentence, telling lunchtime friends
that this had been his morning's work,
then meeting them again for dinner
to announce that he had put it back.

THE RHYME

Searching for the rhyme
what he found gazed back
with a look of reproach
as if to say *About time.*
What took you so long?
But even then he shied away
and didn't choose it.

Not that it was wrong,
just far too right
for him to admit
the truth of the pain
it might have brought,
and so to his shame
he stepped aside
to take a safer route.

WORD BY WORD

Whatever you think you might be
about to say let the language
go all out for it word by word
like scattering seeds at random
in a wilderness then bed them
purposefully down. Who knows
but this may become the garden
you always had in mind, a groundplan
bent on emergence long before
you found the form that chance
would have you take. Look now
at what you've done, the pattern
of your planting word by word
into this sonnet language made.

FROM THE KITCHEN WINDOW

Two pigeons strutting
among indifferent sparrows
clatter at take-off.

A tenacious wren
clings to the hanging feeder
that swings and rattles.

These have become
my feathered avatars
now that I'm alone,

gone with the wind
or hanging in there still
depending on the weather.

GLASS HOUSES

People in glass houses
should not throw stones

nor should they shift ground
while standing to reason.

So little could shatter
their window on the world

that these words of caution
are best not ignored.

                    *

What passes outside
is light reflected

or the dazzle of darkness
in silhouette.

All of it only
a stone's throw away

but life as it is
without intervention.

FULL CIRCLE

Are we there yet?
was childhood's cry

from a back seat
on the outward journey:

her pearl-tipped finger
tracing the route-map,

his gloved hands
steady on the wheel.

                    *

Not yet but nearly
is age's answer

as he drives alone
along the homeward stretch,

now with an empty
seat beside him

and only his luggage
lying in the back.

MOVING ON

Let's cross that bridge
when we come to it, you said

not noticing
we'd crosssed already

and were
none the wiser,

holding each other
as we had before.

       *

So we moved on,
our shadows in the river

biding their time
until the sun came out

to bring them to the surface
gazing back at us

as if in wonderment
through parted clouds.